The GALAXY GUIDES

COULD WE SURVIVE ON OTHER PLANETS?

Alix Wood

PowerKiDS press

Published in 2016 by **Rosen Publishing**
29 East 21ˢᵗ Street, New York, NY 10010

Editor: Eloise Macgregor
Designer: Alix Wood
Consultant: Kevin E. Yates, Fellow of the Royal Astronomical Society

Photo Credits: Cover, 1, 4, 8-9, 14, 15, 19, 20, 21 top, 22, 24-25, 26, 27 bottom © NASA; 5 © Alix Wood; 6, 7, 12, 13, 21 main image, 23 top © Dollar Photo Club; 10 © Gregory H. Revera; 11 top © B Critchley/ Dreamstime; 11 middle © Don Davis; 11 bottom © Alix Wood; 16 © NASA Ames/JPL-Caltech/T Pyle; 17 © NASA/Matipon Tangmatitham; NASA/Science Source Images; 23 bottom © Shutterstock

Cataloging-in-Publication Data

Wood, Alix.
Could we survive on other planets? / by Alix Wood.
p. cm. — (The galaxy guides)
Includes index.
ISBN 978-1-4994-0867-6 (pbk.)
ISBN 978-1-4994-0866-9 (6 pack)
ISBN 978-1-4994-0865-2 (library binding)
1. Space astronomy — Juvenile literature.
2. Planets — Juvenile literature. I. Wood, Alix. II. Title.
QB602.W66 2016
523.4—d23

Manufactured in the United States of America

CPSIA Compliance Information: Batch #: WS15PK
For Further Information contact Rosen Publishing, New York, New York at 1-800-237-9932

Contents

Could People Live on Other Planets?

Our **solar system** is made up of a number of planets that go around the Sun. Space scientists have found more than 500 other solar systems and are discovering new ones every year. There may be tens of billions of solar systems in our galaxy! Could any of these other planets become our home?

In our solar system, each planet goes around the Sun following its own circular path, called an **orbit**. Each planet is very different. Some are mainly made of gas, some are rocky, and most have no breathable air or water. Some are so close to the Sun that they are too hot. Some are too far away and are too cold. Earth is a perfect **habitat** for life as it has water, breathable air, and is not too cold or too hot.

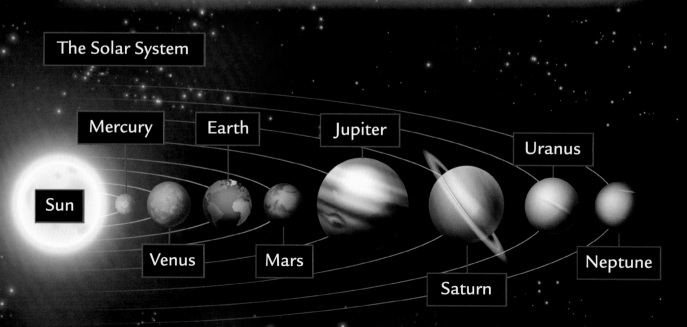

The Solar System

Sun

Mercury

Venus

Earth

Mars

Jupiter

Saturn

Uranus

Neptune

Scientists are looking at other planets to see if we could live on them. We might be able to live on other objects in our solar system, such as moons and **asteroids**, too. Scientists are also looking at other distant solar systems to see if they can find a planet like Earth there. You would think it would be easy to find another place to live if there are tens of billions of other solar systems! The reality is that it is not easy at all.

Scientists are looking for three things a planet needs so it can support life:

1) a planet with gases such as **oxygen** that could support life

2) a planet with water

3) a planet that's not too cold or too hot

HANDS-ON SCIENCE

What Do Plants Need to Survive?

You will need: 4 identical plants (grow some cress, or buy some from a store), paper and pen, water

All our food comes from plants. We eat plants and the animals we eat eat plants. Find out what plants would need on our new planet to survive. Take two plants and put them on a windowsill. Label one plant "water." Water this plant when the soil feels dry. Don't water the other plant. Put the other two plants in a dark cupboard. Label one plant "water." Water this plant when the soil feels dry and leave the other one. Which plant looks the healthiest after two weeks? Why do you think it does?

water

How Do Living Things Survive on Earth?

Earth is home to all kinds of living things, from the most basic **microorganisms** to complex forms of life such as humans. What makes Earth such a good planet for life?

Its Atmosphere

Most animal life on Earth breathes the oxygen in our **atmosphere**. Our atmosphere protects life on Earth from the Sun's harmful radiation, too. Earth's atmosphere is held in place by **gravity**. Gravity is a force where objects with a large **mass** pull other objects toward them. Earth's gravity pulls the atmosphere toward it. Small planets such as Mercury don't have enough gravity to keep strong **solar winds** from destroying their atmospheres.

Its Climate

Earth's atmosphere contains a little **carbon dioxide** too. This gas helps keep Earth's mild temperature. It traps heat so the Sun's energy doesn't all leak back out into space. If it weren't for this, much of Earth's oceans would freeze and many species would die.

Its Water

Water is very important. All life we know of needs water. Earth has water as seas, oceans, lakes, ice, and in our clouds. Other planets don't have water in liquid form.

Its Light

Although all planets get light from the Sun, on Earth it helps things grow. Plants produce oxygen. If we could get plants to grow on another planet they would help the planet's atmosphere by adding oxygen. The planet would also have to receive sunlight regularly. Some planets, like Venus, take so long to spin around on their **axis** that parts of the planet are in darkness for a long time. Venus takes 243 days to spin on its axis.

Its Sun

Without the Sun there would be no life on Earth. Earth is the ideal distance from the Sun, so it gets the right amount of heat and light. Also, the Sun's gravity keeps Earth in its orbit. Without the Sun, Earth would float away.

Why Do We Need to Live on Other Planets?

I t would take a lot of effort to find a planet that we could live on, and to get ourselves there. Why would we ever want to do that?

Earth may not always be a good place to live. The Sun is gradually getting larger. In around two billion years Earth will become too hot to live on. In three and a half billion years our oceans will start to boil. That's a very long way into the future, but scientists are already starting to plan ahead!

the Sun gradually getting larger

We are using up Earth's resources fast. We may have to leave to find other food or energy. We might leave Earth simply to conserve it, too. Our planet could become a kind of nature reserve that we visit now and again.

Earth Collision!

NASA estimates there are around a thousand asteroids that are larger than 0.62 miles (1 km) in diameter. The smallest of these hit Earth roughly every 500,000 years. A large asteroid hit was believed to have wiped out the dinosaurs 65 million years ago. We either need to learn how to prevent the asteroids from hitting Earth, or we need to find a new home.

Space scientists believe that the Andromeda galaxy and our galaxy, the **Milky Way**, will collide in around four and a half billion years. The Andromeda galaxy is approaching the Milky Way at approximately 60 to 85 miles (100 to 140 km) per second! Don't worry, it's still a very long way away though!

Our own actions may destroy Earth. A deadly man-made **virus** or nuclear weapons could have the power to destroy life on Earth. If people could start life on another planet, and take all our knowledge with us, then our civilization would survive for millions more years.

The Moon is our closest object in space. People have already walked on the surface of the Moon. There are many reasons why living there would be very difficult for people, though.

Reasons for and Against Living on the Moon

FOR

The Moon is our closest neighbor. The Apollo astronauts made the trip in three days.

The Moon would be a good base from which to launch rockets to explore other planets.

We could test if humans could survive in low gravity. If they could, we could move to other planets.

Communication between the Moon and Earth is quite easy.

We could grow crops at the Moon's north pole, which has continuous sunlight all summer.

You can see Earth from the Moon, helping people feel close to home.

AGAINST

We would need oxygen to breathe.

In most areas the nights are long and the temperature is very cold.

The Moon may have ice under the surface, but it would be very hard to get at.

Transporting the things we would need would be expensive.

The Moon's low gravity, and solar winds and **solar flares** from the Sun, may all harm people's health.

The Moon has no protective atmosphere, so there is more chance of being hit by a high-speed **micrometeoroid**, which can cause damage even though they are tiny.

a view inside a donut-shaped city design

Japan, Russia, and the US all have plans to create a base on the Moon in the next few years. There have been many different design ideas for a place people could live in. A donut-shaped city was designed to gently spin to create the effect of gravity. Newer ideas include creating a shelter in one of the large pits on the Moon's surface.

HANDS-ON SCIENCE

Design Your Own Moon City

You will need: Paper, pencils, and imagination!

Could you design your own Moon city? These are some of the things you need to think about:

gravity   The low gravity on the Moon means everything floats around

weather   Will there be enough sunshine? Will it be too hot or too cold?

atmosphere   Will people be able to breathe?

protection   People need protection from the solar winds, micrometeoroids, solar flares, and harmful rays of the Sun.

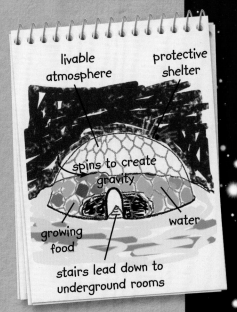

livable atmosphere

protective shelter

spins to create gravity

water

growing food

stairs lead down to underground rooms

Which Planets Could We Live On?

Which planet in our solar system would be the best to choose to live on? None are exactly the same as Earth, and all have some problems. Some are so cold there is no chance of life!

VENUS

Venus is the hottest planet. With its clouds of **acid** and atmosphere of poisonous gas it would not make a good home! It is a similar size to Earth and has similar gravity, though. The pressure of its atmosphere would crush a person instantly!

Score 3/5

MERCURY

Mercury is the closest planet in our solar system to the Sun. It is very hot in the day and freezing cold at night. It has no atmosphere, no moon, and little gravity.

Score 2/5

Neptune

Venus

Mars

Jupiter

Saturn

Uranus

Mercury

Earth

MARS

Mars is the fourth planet from the Sun. It's about half the size of Earth. It is the second closest planet to Earth. Mars has north and south poles covered with ice made from carbon dioxide and water.

Score 4/5

JUPITER

Jupiter is the largest planet. It is mostly made of gas and has a very thick atmosphere. It has no solid surface that we could live on. Its atmosphere is very hot.

Score 2/5

URANUS

Uranus is made of gas and has no solid surface. Its seasons are extreme. It is even colder than Saturn. Gravity at the surface is similar to Earth's.

Score 2/5

SATURN

Saturn is the second largest planet. It has rings made of rock and ice. The planet itself is made of gas and has no solid surface. Gravity at the surface is about the same as on Earth. There is some water on Saturn and water ice in its rings. It is far too cold for people to live on.

Score 2/5

NEPTUNE

Neptune is larger than Earth but has a similar gravity at the surface. It is a long way from the Sun so it is extremely cold. It is very windy. It has seasons that last for 40 years. At the poles it has either complete darkness or daylight for 40 years at a time!

Score 1/5

Could People Live on Mars?

Mars is our closest planet. It is still over 48 million miles (77.2 million km) away though! It takes around nine months to get there. Scientists are studying Mars to see if it has ever had life on it.

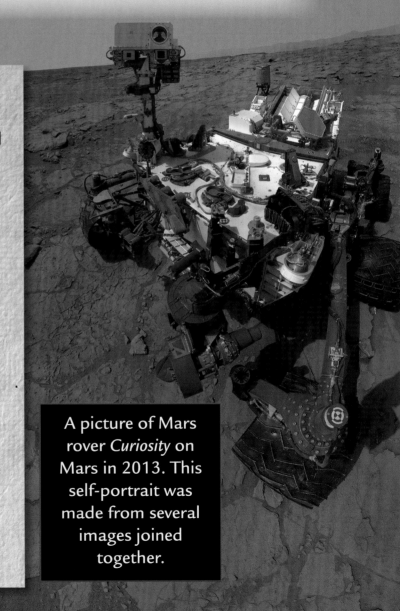

A picture of Mars rover *Curiosity* on Mars in 2013. This self-portrait was made from several images joined together.

FACT FILE

Mars Rovers

A Mars rover is an automated vehicle. Scientists use them to move across the surface of Mars collecting samples and photographs. Rovers can be directed from Earth. Operators can move the rover to examine anything interesting they see. They can park the rover in a sunny place over the winter, too. The scientists are searching for evidence of ancient life, and evidence of water. They are also studying the rock to see what it is made of. They want to see if humans could live there one day.

It takes around 20 minutes for signals from Earth to reach a remote control vehicle on Mars, so operators can't command the vehicle from Earth while watching it. If a command to stop took too long to reach the rover it could crash. Instead they must plan the route the rover is to travel, and then program the rover.

Program a Mars Rover

You will need: a friend, a large sandy or paved area, some chalk or a stick, pen and paper

On the ground, draw a grid of squares using chalk, or a stick if on sand. This is the surface of Mars. Put crosses in some of the squares to be obstacles like craters or rocks. Draw the same grid on your piece of paper. Write down the instructions you would need to give to your "Mars rover" friend. You want instructions like "Forward one square. Right two squares." Now see if you can get your rover across the surface of Mars safely. Turn around so you can't see your friend and read out the instructions. Then turn back around and see if your rover made it safely!

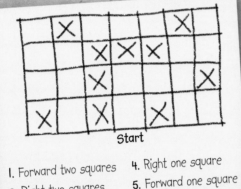

Start

1. Forward two squares
2. Right two squares
3. Forward one square
4. Right one square
5. Forward one square

Life on Earth needs water to live. Scientists can tell if Mars ever had water by studying things like how the surface is shaped. The forces of wind and water change a landscape. This is how places like the Grand Canyon were made. There is a canyon that is even bigger on Mars. It is so big it would stretch from one side of the U.S. to the other. How was this canyon created? Could it have been made by a river too? There is evidence of small quantities of salty water flowing on Mars. This may mean there was once life on Mars, so maybe there could be still.

Could We Live in Another Solar System?

The Sun is one of billions of stars in our galaxy, the Milky Way. There are billions of other galaxies in the Universe, but their planets would be too far away for us to travel to. Scientists are searching for planets in other solar systems within the Milky Way.

In 2009, NASA launched a spacecraft called Kepler. Kepler's mission is to search for **exoplanets** that may have life on them. An exoplanet is any planet outside our solar system. Scientists want to find planets like Earth. Earth orbits our Sun at just the right distance so our water hasn't frozen or boiled. Scientists call planets that perfect distance from their stars "Goldilocks planets" after the girl who wanted her porridge the perfect temperature!

FACT FILE

What Is Kepler?

Kepler is a big telescope. It sends images back to Earth. It has the largest camera ever launched into space. It points to the same distant part of the Milky Way, examining the stars, for four years.

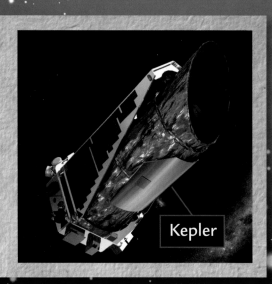
Kepler

Kepler finds distant planets by noticing tiny changes in a star's brightness. The changes shows that a planet may be moving in front of its star. To be sure the change is really caused by a planet, Kepler must see it repeated regularly, just like Earth orbits the Sun once every year. That's why Kepler watches the same stars for four years! Scientists measure the temperature of the star by examining its light. They also measure how far the planet is from its star. If the distance is just right, it might be a Goldilocks planet!

Kepler-22 is a star in the Milky Way too faint to be seen with the naked eye. In 2011, scientists discovered a Goldilocks planet orbiting it. They called it Kepler-22b. It is the first Earth-sized planet found at the right distance from a star. Could we live there?

Kepler-22b

Can Anything Live Without Water?

Everything on Earth needs water to survive. Not everything drinks water, some life gets its water from its food. Life on our planet is all made up of cells, and cells need water. There may be some other form of life on another planet that has evolved differently, and so would not require water for life, but not on Earth.

Of all the animals on Earth, a tiny **arthropod** called the tardigrade is probably the most likely to survive on another planet. They can survive for ten years without water! They can dry out and then **rehydrate** themselves. They can survive temperatures below freezing and above boiling point. They can survive very low and high pressures, and dangerous radiation. In 2011 some tardigrades were placed outside an orbiting space shuttle as an experiment, and survived!

Tardigrades are only about 0.02 inch (0.5 mm) long. They are short and plump with four pairs of legs.

Do Other Planets Have Anything Like Water?

Venus

It's possible alien life could survive on other fluids similar to water. Liquid **methane** and **ammonia** can behave like water. Carbon dioxide can become liquid when heated to extremes and under high pressure, too. Some scientists believe carbon dioxide in this state might be able to support life. Venus's atmosphere is around 97 percent carbon dioxide and has the perfect pressure and temperature conditions to make carbon dioxide act like a liquid.

When we think of "life" we can only imagine species we are familiar with here on Earth. Because of this, we think water is essential, because all life on Earth needs water. But some forms of life could use materials that we do not know about yet. There are still many things that we do not know. Life-forms could also live in unusual places, such as under the surface of planets. Life could even be in a form that we cannot notice with the senses that we have.

Could We Make Our Own World to Live On?

If we can't find the perfect planet, or it is too expensive to get there, could we create our own world? It would be pretty impossible to build a planet, but perhaps people could create a large spaceship.

Do People Live in Space Now?

People live on the International Space Station (ISS). People have been living there since November 2000. Between two and seven people are on the space station at any one time. The ISS is the biggest object ever flown in space. It travels around Earth at 17,100 miles (27,600 km) per hour. At that speed it completes 15.5 orbits per day, so the crew sees a sunrise or sunset every 92 minutes!

The ISS (right) can be seen at night. It looks like a slow, bright white dot. Look at the NASA website to see when it next flies over your area!

People are looking at developing spacecraft that will allow more people to live permanently in space. The spacecraft are designed to spin to create their own gravity. Up to now, designs similar to this donut-shaped craft could only house around 500 people. It would be difficult to make a spacecraft that could be home to everyone on our planet!

HANDS-ON SCIENCE

Test If You Can Eat in Zero Gravity

You will need: some applesauce, a spoon, a wall, a pillow, an adult

Living with no gravity means everything floats around! Have you ever wondered how astronauts swallow food? Try for yourself! Instead of zero gravity, try to swallow upside down by standing on your head. Put a pillow next to the wall and get into a headstand. Ask an adult to spoon some applesauce into your mouth. Can you swallow the food? You and astronauts can swallow food because your muscles push the food to your stomach.

Is There Alien Life in Space?

In our solar system, most scientists agree that life on another planet wouldn't look like aliens in the movies. Life-forms would probably be very small and look like bugs! Experts also think aliens wouldn't live outside. The conditions in space are too harsh. Missions will be looking underground, too.

Single-celled microorganisms were the first forms of life to develop on Earth. Although they don't look like much, finding one on another planet would be very exciting. It would mean that life has evolved in at least one other place in our solar system, which suggests life could be common throughout the Universe!

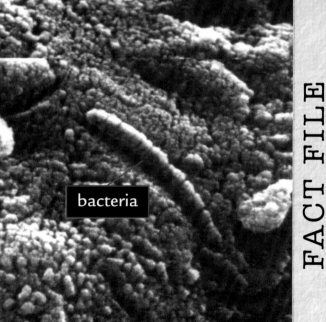

bacteria

FACT FILE

Meet Allen Hills 84001 and the Microorganism From Mars!

Microorganisms can hide in rocks to protect themselves against extreme conditions. A piece of a meteorite was found at the South Pole. Allen Hills 84001, as the meteorite is known, is believed to have come from Mars 16 million years ago. Some scientists believe it has a fossil of bacteria in it (left). Not everyone agrees though. Scientists are reasonably sure that the fossil was created before it landed on Earth. Is this proof of life on Mars?

HANDS-ON SCIENCE

Grow Your Own Bacteria!

You will need: flavorless gelatin, a glass jar and lid, a refrigerator, a stove, a pan, some water, an adult

Ask an adult to help you. Boil some water in a pan. Place the jar and lid in the boiling water for one minute. This will kill any bacteria. Make up the gelatin according to the package's instructions. Pour the gelatin into the jar, put on the lid, and place in the fridge overnight. Remove the jar lid and touch the gelatin. Put the lid back on and leave the jar somewhere warm for a few days. You will see some white spots appear on the gelatin. These are your skin's bacteria! Microorganisms are so tiny we usually can't see them. Using the gelatin as food, these have bred in the jar until there are so many we can see them!

Is Earth being visited by aliens from outside our solar system, like we see in the movies? Probably not. Most apparent sightings of spacecraft have a logical explanation. They were new aircraft, military equipment, or even people pretending to be aliens. People will keep on looking. We just may not have searched in the right place yet!

Are We Trying to Make Contact with Aliens?

I f there is any intelligent life out in space, should we try to contact them? Some people aren't sure whether contacting them would be a good idea. They may not be friendly. Contact also is not easy. Aliens would be unlikely to understand any of our human languages.

People have tried to send messages to space for years. Some people thought drawing large shapes in the desert would be understood as a sign of civilization. Others thought that sending numbers would act like a universal language. One of the main ways we have tried sending messages is by using radio telescopes like these below.

SETI (the Search for Extra Terrestrial Intelligence)

If there is alien life, a space program called SETI might find it. Since 1959 the project has searched for radio signals from intelligent life in space. Using radio telescopes they look for special patterns in radio waves which could have been sent by a civilization in space. Radio waves can travel through the thick clouds of gas and dust in space, and can be used both day and night. They send radio signals into space too. They hope that they may one day reach another civilization in space. So far they've heard nothing, but that may be because the equipment is not good enough yet. It is possible that a civilization has heard our signals, and is sending their reply to us now. The only way we'll know is to keep looking and listening.

HANDS-ON SCIENCE

Send a Message to Space

Two Voyager spacecraft carry gold-plated gramophone records of the sounds of nature, music, and greetings from several languages. The covers were engraved with images and directions for how to use the record. They are both floating out in space now. What do you think aliens would want to know about Earth? Try to design your own CD and CD cover.

Some of SETI's radio telescopes

Can Ordinary People Go to Space?

It is very expensive to send people into space. It also can be very dangerous. Most people that have been into space are highly trained astronauts. Some ordinary people have now been to space, though. And in the future, more people will get the opportunity to space travel.

Dennis Anthony Tito, an American multimillionaire, was the first space tourist to pay for his own trip into space. Mark Shuttleworth (below) a South African businessman, was the second space tourist. He paid around 20 million dollars to go on the trip! He spent eight days helping with experiments on the International Space Station. Shuttleworth had one year of training and preparation before he was allowed on the trip.

Mark Shuttleworth (left) on the Russian Soyuz spacecraft, docking at the International Space Station

Many companies are beginning to offer **suborbital** space flights. Suborbital means the craft goes into space, but does not complete a full orbit of Earth. One company, Virgin Galactic, has already sold tickets worth $200,000 dollars each to go on their first flights.

HANDS-ON SCIENCE

Could You Be an Astronaut?

Teamwork and puzzle-solving are important skills if you want to be an astronaut. Try this puzzle test and see if you would make the grade.

You will need: An old jigsaw puzzle (around 30 pieces), 2 pairs of thick gloves, a friend, a pen, a table

Turn the jigsaw pieces upside down and, using the pen, mark all the edge pieces with an "A" and the inside pieces with a "B." Shuffle the pieces up and share them between you and your friend on the floor. Put on your thick gloves. Both select all your pieces that have an "A" and take them to the table. Put all the jigsaw edges together. Then go back to the floor and pick up all the "B" pieces. Head back to the table and see how quickly you can complete the puzzle.

Galaxy Quiz

Are you a galaxy genius? Test your skills with this quiz and see if you know your aliens from your microorganisms!

1. Which of these statements is correct?
   a) an orbit is a circular path around an object
   b) an orbit is a tool used on a spacecraft

2. What does most animal life on Earth breathe in?
   a) carbon dioxide
   b) hydrogen
   c) oxygen

3. A microorganism is
   a) a very small spacecraft
   b) a very basic life-form
   c) a computer

4. Which of these planets is closest to us?
   a) Mars
   b) Neptune
   c) Saturn

5. What is a Mars rover?
   a) a dog that lives on Mars
   b) a spacecraft
   c) a vehicle used to move around the surface of Mars

6. What is our galaxy called?
   a) Andromeda
   b) The Milky Way
   c) Pinwheel

7. People live in space now on the International Space Station.
   a) true
   b) false

8. What does SETI do?
   a) search for intelligent life in space
   b) build spacecraft
   c) train astronauts

9. Which of these things is essential for human life?
   a) electricity
   b) water
   c) cars

10. Which of these statements is correct?
   a) People could never live on another planet.
   b) People may be able to live on another planet if we find
      one with the right conditions.

Glossary

acid (A-sid)
Something that breaks down matter faster than water does.

ammonia (uh-MO-nyuh)
A colorless gas, made of nitrogen and hydrogen, with a strong smell.

arthropod (AR-thruh-pod)
The scientific name for an animal with jointed legs and a hard outer covering.

asteroids (AS-teh-roydz)
Bodies of rock and iron left over from when the main planets formed. They are in orbit around the Sun.

atmosphere (AT-muh-sfeer)
The gases around an object in space. On Earth this is air.

axis (AK-sus)
A straight line on which an object turns or seems to turn.

carbon dioxide (KAHR-bun dy-OK-syd)
An odorless, colorless gas. People breathe out carbon dioxide.

exoplanet (ek-so-PLA-net)
A planet that does not orbit the Sun and instead orbits a different star.

gravity (GRA-vih-tee)
The force that causes objects to move toward each other. The more mass an object has, the more gravity it has.

habitat (HA-buh-tat)
The kind of land where an animal or a plant naturally lives.

mass (MAS) The amount of matter in something.

methane (MEH-thayn)
A common gas in the solar system. On Earth, it is found in natural gas.

micrometeroid (my-kroh-MEE-tee-uh-royd)
A small particle of rock in space.

microorganisms (my-kroh-OR-guh-nih-zumz)
Very tiny living things.

Milky Way (MIL-kee WAY)
A galaxy containing hundreds of billions of stars, one of which is our Sun.

NASA (NA-suh)
National Aeronautics and Space Administration, the United States' space agency.

orbit (OR-bit) A circular path.

oxygen (OK-sih-jen)
A gas that has no color or taste that people and animals breathe.

rehydrate (ree-HY-drayt)
To refill with water.

solar flare (SOH-ler FLAYR)
An explosion on the Sun's surface that gives off a lot of energy.

solar system (SOH-ler SIS-tem)
The Sun, along with all the planets and other objects that are bound to it by gravity.

solar winds (SOH-ler WINDZ)
Tiny pieces of charged matter that flow from the Sun.

suborbital (sub-OR-bih-tul)
Falling short of a complete orbit.

virus (VY-rus) Something tiny that causes a disease.

Further Information

Books

Dyson, Marianne J. *Home on the Moon: Living on a Space Frontier.* Des Moines, IA: National Geographic Children's Books, 2003.

Portman, Michael. *Could We Live on Other Planets?* New York, NY: Gareth Stevens Publishing, 2014.

Due to the changing nature of Internet links, PowerKids Press has developed an online list of websites related to the subject of this book. This site is updated regularly. Please use this link to access the list: **www.powerkidslinks.com/tgg/other**

Index

Answers
1. a)
2. c)
3. b)
4. a)
5. c)
6. b)
7. a)
8. a)
9. b)
10. b)